RUNNING

Written By:
Herbert I. Kavet

Illustrated By:
Martin Riskin

Ivory Tower Publishing Co., Inc.
125 Walnut Street
P.O. Box 9132
Watertown, MA 02272-9132
Telephone #: (617) 923-1111   Fax #: (617) 923-8839

With 100 yards to go, Warren pulls ahead of the
surprised Kenyans and the crowd goes wild.

Which Running Shoes Are Best For You?

When running shoes were called sneakers, they cost $3.95. Now, before you buy them you have to decide if you pronate or supinate, whatever that is, and answer embarrassing questions like how far you run each week, what you weigh and whether they're for racing or training (light or heavy training) — when all you're really interested in is if they match your new aqua sweat suit.

Phil breaks down and decides to throw out his 1983 training shoes.

No matter how much Felix ran each week, at a party
someone always upstaged him.

Marilyn tried hard to understand her new sport's language:
10K, 43:20, 5K, pronate, Fartlik, repeat sprints, tapering,
peaking, lateral stability, shin splints, cross training.

Dressing For The Cold

The proper way to dress for cold weather running is so you'll be chilly for the first mile. Following this theory, by the time my first mile is reached, my core body temperature is approaching hypothermia and my feet are barely moving (no advice is forthcoming for people who only want to run one mile). Much better is to dress nice and warm and then leave the extra sweat shirt, hat and gloves in a friend's mailbox along your route. I had one of my favorite hats mailed to Alaska this way, but if you remember to drive by and pick them up later, it works fine.

No matter how hot it is, some idiot is
running in a sweat suit.
No matter how cold it is, another is in shorts.

"I finish my 3 mile loop about the time Rob finishes his stretching."

Toilets And Races

No one admits to being nervous before a race; after all, this is just for fun, right? But somehow there seems to be a 20 minute wait for every Port-a-Potty at the start of every race. Can all these people just be going inside to adjust their underwear? At any given starting gun, 20% of the competitors are still waiting in line to go to the toilet. If this problem could somehow be solved, you wouldn't believe how many people would improve their 10K and marathon times.

"Let's see, 2,000 competitors—I guess three
Port-a-Potties is about right."

"Since I've started running with Fang, I've had no trouble from other dogs."

"I don't run with anyone who carries a stop watch."

Dogs

That lovable puppy who jumps up and licks your face when you visit turns into a raging beast when you run by its house in your neon shorts. Some say the animal is protecting its territory but no runner believes that. The reason dogs attack runners is because they smell fear on them and they want to strike before the runner comes to his or her senses, realizes that they're bigger than the dog, and picks up a stout rolled newspaper.

"So this new guy says, 'I always run with my attack cat.' "

"Bran's cutting in a little early today, eh Joel?"

It only starts to rain when you're at the furthest point from your home.

How To "Go" In The Outdoors

Every runner experiences this overwhelming urge every now and then, if you know what I mean, brought on by the morning coffee or jiggling rhythm of the run. The first signs start to radiate up from your middle shortly after you leave home. It's close enough to turn back but you figure expelling a little gas will relieve the pressure and you can finish your workout. Then half way into your run, without a tree in sight, disaster strikes. Only then do you understand the advantages of darkness provided by pre-dawn or evening runs.

How To "Go" In The Outdoors

1. The no-handed pointing at birds. (Men Only)
2. The between parked cars desperation squat.
3. The poison ivy regret.
4. The back against a tree hope you miss your pants gambit.

"The idea really is to hydrate before and during the race."

"I just can't stand women who show off."

The Runner's Wave

In some places like Eugene, Oregon or Boulder, Colorado, runners WAVE to each other and smile in passing. In other places like large Eastern cities, the same wave can get you arrested. "Officer, this pervert tried to attack me in the park." But mostly the runner's wave is a friendly nod of kinship towards some other suffering fool, as they run in the opposite direction.

Herman finds it easy to do 6 minute miles when his route takes him through the South Bronx.

"You can outrun the mosquitoes, but those green-headed flies will eat your head off."

Bill finds his "good luck" socks sometimes offend
other competitors.

Repairing Running Shoes

Every now and then I read about some sort of special goo that you squeeze on your running shoe bottoms to repair them. Who would want to repair a running shoe? Every 30 minutes a new super improved model appears promising to propel you to even greater speeds with a boron compound sole and compressed gases and to cushion you with gel or air and stabilize you with dual density mid-sole arches and ultra cushion shock absorbers. All this for maybe $169.00 and you're supposed to throw them out after 6 months because the bounce has gone out of them?

"Well, those are my training shoes and those are my lightweight racers and those, my long distance racers and those, my rainy day sloggers and those, last year's racing shoes, and those are my extra support training shoes."

"Ben only runs like that when he has to use a toilet."

Gary's accidental use of Gatorade to cool off annoys him throughout the race.

Runners' Hand Signals

That's what I think
of runners
who pass me.

I heard this was
an obscene gesture
in some third world
countries.

I wish this booger
would dry and
fall off.

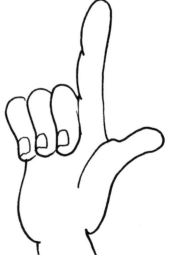

Runners' Hand Signals

I think I'm
having a
heart attack.

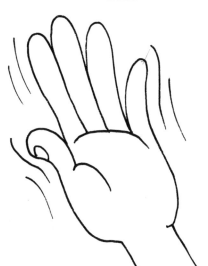

You're about done,
you lucky stiff,
and I'm just
starting.

I'm about done,
and you,
you poor sucker,
have 3 miles to go.

"Burt's training log says he ran 27 miles last week, but he really ran 24."

Heart Monitors

These devices are great to wear when you're running. First of all, when they are working, which is about half the time, it's a great reassurance that your heart is still ticking and you are still alive. Then again, if you're really working up a sweat and pouring on the steam, it lets you know if your heart is helping or just shirking its duty. The beep, beep, beeping can drive your running partner nuts and that's pretty cool, also. The sophisticated models of these devices tell you when you're working too hard, when you're loafing, and when it's time to go home and eat potato chips.

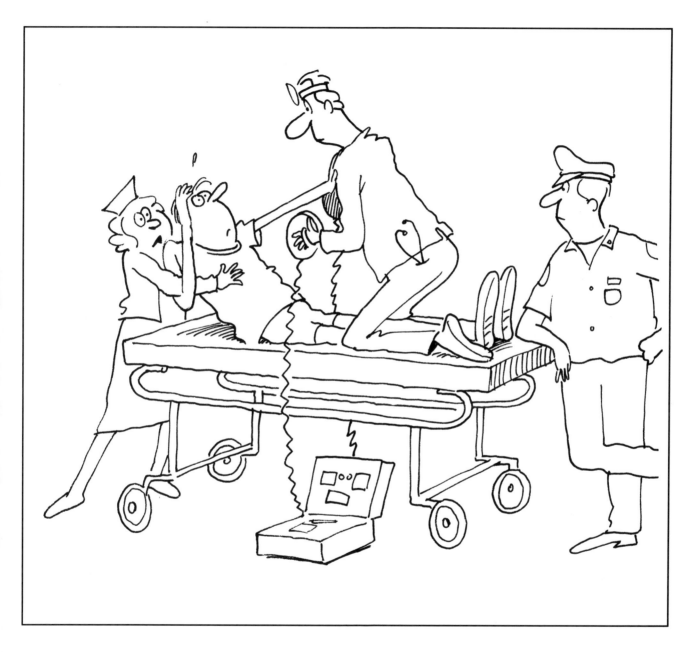

John realizes it was only his heart monitor batteries wearing out.

"Decided to take a rest day, I see."

"You're quite serious about your running, aren't you, Kathy?"

Fashions For Running

The best fashion for running is T-shirts from major races, the farther away the better. "Oh, I see you did the Tokyo Marathon — bitch of a course, wasn't it?" You figure he's lying and you know you bought the shirt at a K-Mart, but it'll definitely fool novice runners. If you can't find these T-shirts, it's mandatory to at least wear one that promotes some running shoe company in letters at least six inches high.

"I can't stand the cyclists."

"That's not fair."

The carbo loaders arrive at the all-you-can-eat
pasta buffet.

Where To Run

Runners throughout history have been carrying out this quest for an all downhill loop. The flat loop is attainable in most places, but the all downhill run remains elusive, though not impossible. Most people who succeed in running downhill loops have very nice wives, husbands, or friends who pick them up and drive them home from the bottom.

Rachel beats her dad home for the first time.

Marsha decides to take up running to help lose
weight, but figures it's best to carbo load first.

Harris hoped he'd get to meet lots of girls running.

Calories And Running

Running is a good way to lose weight. For every 3500 calories burned, you lose a pound. If you want to lose 5 pounds just run from, say, Boston to New York. It won't work if you have peanuts and beer on the way home.

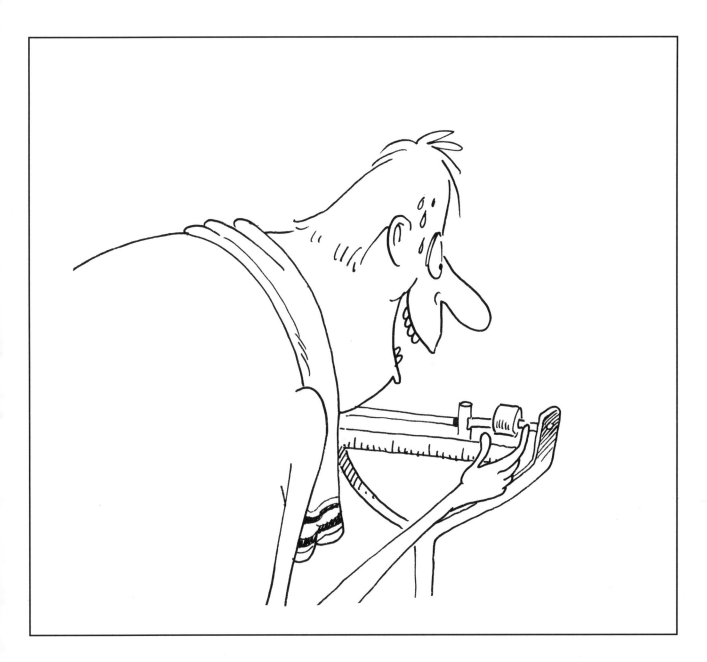

"Sure enough, this morning's run took off
2 ounces."

Calories And Running

Activity	Calories Burned
Per Mile Run	180 Calories
Per dog encountered	add 36 Calories
Per call of nature stop	add 22 Calories
If no bushes available	add 57 Calories
Running with attractive member of opposite sex	add 20 Calories

Running into woods with
    attractive member
    of opposite sex
	add 120 Calories

Calories And Running

Running Activity	Calories Burned
Stretching	8 Calories
Washing running outfit	26 Calories
Washing after 26 weeks of use	140 Calories

Of course, some running activities add calories.

Activity	Calories Burned
3 beers to replace liquids	+270 Calories
Potato chips for salt loss	+400 Calories
Chocolate bars for energy	+625 Calories

The last of the Mohicans.

"Come on, Sam, those new shoes weren't
that expensive."

Running And Health

As everyone knows, running improves your cardiovascular system as much as 96%

Your Psychological Well Being	72%
Your Concentration	29%
Your Skin Tone	18%

and reduces your probability of cancer, heart attacks, and other horrible diseases by 45%.

Running And Health

Running also <u>increases</u> your chances of being run over by a large truck by 600%.

Being partially eaten by a large dog	+ 425%
Meeting a dangerous mugger	+ 210%
Frostbite on unmentionable parts of your body	+ 500%
Being shouted at by speeding car	+5600%
Stepping in dog doo	+ 760%

The Kenyans' childhood games prepare them for successful careers as marathon runners.

"Gerry is such a sore loser."

"I just knew Sam's running was going to come in handy some day."

Bugs Runners Should Avoid

Bernstein's Chafing Mite

The microscopic mites move in large packs and seek out the inside of a sweaty thigh. They quickly take up residence in the area and have a block party drinking and carousing and doing the shuffle. This dance irritates the tender white flesh on the inner crotch and thigh and turns it a glowing painful pink.

The Crotch Tick

This evil little creature secretes himself in fabric of unwashed running shorts and hibernates until the soiled shorts are once again used. The running motion wakens the tick and he proceeds to do a mating dance which wouldn't be that bad except that the tick uses two flaming crochet needles in the spectacular finale.

The Earwax Beetle

A roly-poly hard shelled little creature will fly into a crevice in the runner's ear and nestle down for a nap. It is widely thought that the beetle likes the rocking motion of a moving runner.

Bugs Runners Should Avoid

The Red-Eared Nostril Gnat

An insidiously rapid reproducer who will hang around a lamp post or hydrant waiting for an unsuspecting jogger to amble by. The Gnat will quickly fly up the runner's nose and lay enough eggs to populate New York State for 3 years.

Spotted Sneaker Flea

Will attach itself to bottom of a ribbed running shoe and bore upward through the shoe into the runner's foot. The Sneaker Flea will then make a left and take his 2nd right up the leg, pick up an express artery to the neck and lay a big egg just under the skin which will turn into a red hairy boil in 3 weeks.

The Black Mouth Fly

This small virulent Gnat seeks out runners who run with mouths open and flies in and quickly sets up a furnished condominium apartment in victim's throat.

These other books are available at many fine stores.

#2350 Sailing. Using the head at night • Sex & Sailing • Monsters in the Ice Chest • How to look nautical in bars and much more nautical nonsense.

#2351 Computers. Where computers really are made • How to understand computer manuals without reading them • Sell your old $2,000,000 computer for $60 • Why computers are always lonely and much more solid state computer humor.

#2352 Cats. Living with cat hair • The advantages of kitty litter • Cats that fart • How to tell if you've got a fat cat.

#2353 Tennis. Where do lost balls go? • Winning the psychological game • Catching your breath • Perfecting wood shots.

#2354 Bowling. A book of bowling cartoons that covers: Score sheet cheaters • Boozers • Women who show off • Facing your team after a bad box and much more.

#2355 Parenting. Understanding the Tooth Fairy • 1000 ways to toilet train • Informers and tattle tales • Differences between little girls and little boys • And enough other information and laughs to make every parent wet their beds.

#2356 Fitness. T-shirts that will stop them from laughing at you • Earn big money with muscles • Sex and Fitness • Lose weight with laughter from this book.

#2357 Golf. Playing the psychological game • Going to the toilet in the rough • How to tell a real golfer • Some of the best golf cartoons ever printed.

#2358 Fishing. Handling 9" mosquitoes • Raising worms in your microwave oven • Neighborhood targets for fly casting practice • How to get on a first name basis with the Coast Guard plus even more.

#2359 Bathrooms. Why people love their bathroom • Great games to help pass the time on toilets • A frank discussion of bathroom odors • Plus lots of other stuff everyone out of diapers should know.

#2360 Biking. Why the wind is always against you • Why bike clothes are so tight • And lots of other stuff about what goes thunk, thunk, thunk when you pedal.

#2361 Running. How to "go" in the woods • Why running shoes cost more than sneakers • Keeping your lungs from bursting by letting the other guy talk.

Ivory Tower Publishing Co., Inc. 125 Walnut St., PO Box 9132, Watertown, MA 02272-9132
Telephone #: (617) 923-1111   Fax #: (617) 923-8839